Executive Summary

The United States is an Arctic nation[1] through the state of Alaska and its surrounding territorial and Exclusive Economic Zone waters located in and around the Arctic Circle. The United States Navy, as the maritime component of the Department of Defense, has global leadership responsibilities to provide ready forces for current operations and contingency response that include the Arctic Ocean.[2] The Arctic Region[3] remains a challenging operating environment, with a harsh climate, vast distances, and little infrastructure. These issues, coupled with limited operational experience, are just a few substantial challenges the Navy will have to overcome in the Arctic Region. While the Region is expected to remain a low threat security environment where nations resolve differences peacefully, the Navy will be prepared to prevent conflict and ensure national interests are protected.

In the coming decades, the Arctic Ocean will be increasingly accessible and more broadly used by Arctic and non-Arctic nations seeking the Region's abundant resources and trade routes. Due to the significant retreat of sea ice, previously unreachable areas have started to open for maritime use several weeks each year. The predicted rise in oil and gas development, fishing, tourism, and mineral mining could alter the Region's strategic importance as Arctic and non-Arctic nations make investments. Despite this gradual ice opening, the Region's frequent harsh weather and sea conditions are significant limiting factors for Arctic Ocean operations.

This update of the 2009 Navy Arctic Roadmap provides guidance necessary to prepare the Navy to respond effectively to future Arctic Region contingencies, delineates the Navy's leadership role, and articulates the Navy's support to achieve national priorities in the Region. Navy functions in the Arctic Region are no different from those in other maritime regions; however, the Arctic Region environment makes the execution of many of these functions[4] much more challenging.

In May 2013, President Obama published the *National Strategy for the Arctic Region*, defining the desired end state as an Arctic Region stable and free of conflict, where nations act responsibly in a spirit of trust and cooperation, and where economic and energy resources are developed in a sustainable manner. In November 2013, the Secretary of Defense published the *Department of Defense Arctic Strategy*, identifying two supporting objectives to the National Strategy:
- Ensure security, support safety, and promote defense cooperation;
- Prepare for a wide range of challenges and contingencies.

In support of National and Department of Defense aims, the Navy will pursue the following strategic objectives:
- *Ensure United States Arctic sovereignty and provide homeland defense;*
- *Provide ready naval forces* to respond to crisis and contingencies;
- *Preserve freedom of the seas*; and
- *Promote partnerships* within the United States Government and with international allies and partners.

This Roadmap outlines the Navy's strategic approach for the Arctic Region and the ways and means to achieve the desired national end state. Resource constraints and competing near-term mission demands require that naval investments be informed, focused, and deliberate. Proactive planning today allows the Navy to prepare its forces for Arctic Region operations. This Roadmap emphasizes low-cost, long-lead activities that position the Navy to meet future demands. In the near to mid-term, the Navy will concentrate on improving operational capabilities, expertise, and capacity, extending reach, and will leverage interagency and international partners to achieve its strategic objectives. The Roadmap recognizes the need to guide investments by prudently balancing regional requirements with national goals.

This Roadmap provides direction to the Navy for the near-term (present-2020), mid-term (2020-2030), and far-term (beyond 2030), placing particular emphasis on near-term actions necessary to enhance Navy's ability to operate in the Arctic Region in the future. In the near-term, there will be low demand for additional naval involvement in the Region. Current Navy capabilities are sufficient to meet near-term operational needs. Navy will refine doctrine, operating procedures, and tactics, techniques, and procedures to guide future potential operations in the Arctic Region. In the mid-term, the Navy will provide support to the Combatant Commanders, United States Coast Guard, and other United States Government agencies. In the far-term, increased periods of ice-free conditions could require the Navy to expand this support on a more routine basis. Throughout these timeframes, the Navy will continue to develop and enhance cooperative relationships across the Department of Defense, United States Government agencies, industry, and international allies and partners.

The Arctic Ocean

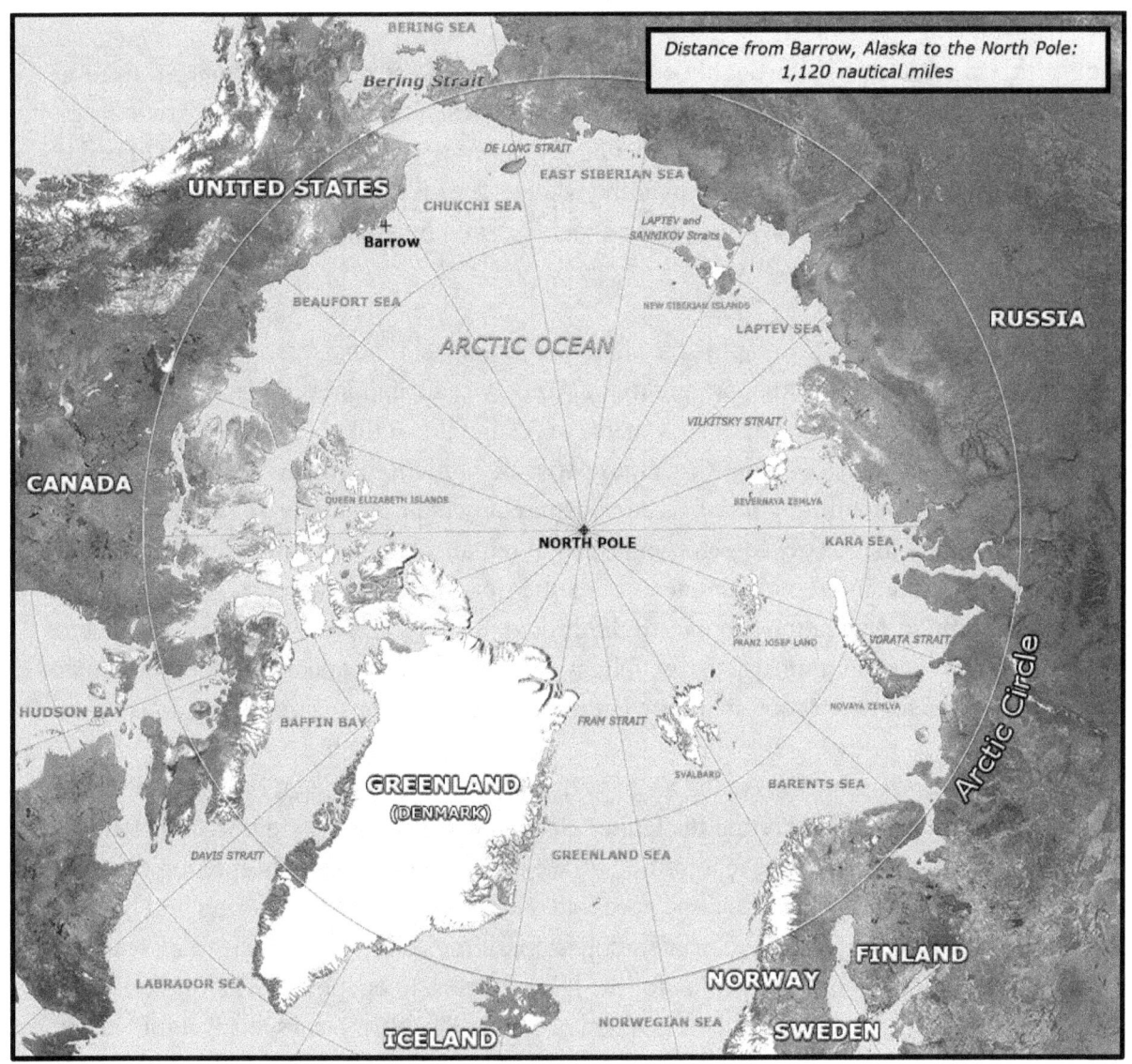

Figure 1: Arctic Ocean (United States Navy graphic)

Introduction

The United States' overarching strategic national security objective for the Arctic Region is a stable and secure region where the national interests of the United States are safeguarded and the homeland is protected.[5] The Navy's primary goal in support of National and Department of Defense aims is to contribute to a peaceful, stable, and conflict-free Arctic Region.

The Arctic Ocean comprises a roughly circular basin and covers an area of about 5.4 million square miles, almost 1.5 times the size of the United States. Today, much of the Arctic Region is ice covered, limiting human access to particular times of the year. The expected continued reduction of multi-year[6]Arctic sea ice over the coming decades will result in increased human activity in the Arctic Ocean. How much of an increase, and in what types of activities, remains to be seen.

The rate of opening of the geography, the short commercial shipping season, the environmental complexities and limitations of operating in the Arctic Ocean, and present geopolitical trends in the Arctic Region lead intelligence assessments to predict it is unlikely the Region will be the site of state-on-state armed conflict. Disputes between Arctic Region nations can be resolved peacefully and without military force, as demonstrated by the Russia-Norway Barents Sea agreement.[7] While the Arctic Region is expected to remain an area of low threat, the United States does have standing security interests in the Region, including threat early warning systems; freedom of navigation and overflight through the region; preventing terrorist attacks against the homeland; combined security obligations with Canada; and deployment of sea and air forces as required for deterrence, maritime presence, and maritime security operations.

As the Arctic Ocean opens, the Bering Strait will have increased strategic importance. This 51-mile wide strait between Russia and the United States, with a depth varying between 98 to 160 feet, represents an important chokepoint for surface and subsurface vessels entering or departing the Arctic Ocean. The Bering Strait and access to and through the Arctic Ocean will become a more important security planning consideration as maritime activity continues to increase. Partnership building opportunities exist for the United States to cooperate with maritime nations as economic activity increases north of the Bering Strait. The Strait has special significance for Russia since it allows Russia to connect her Asian and European naval forces. As the Pacific gateway for Russia's Northern Sea Route, the Bering Strait will become increasingly important for seaborne trade between Europe and Asia. The anticipated increase in traffic through the Strait provides opportunity for the United States to strengthen ties with Russia, promoting maritime security and safety in the region.[8]

For decades, Canada and the United States have been partners in the defense of North America, cooperating within the framework of such instruments as the North Atlantic Treaty Organization (NATO) and North American Aerospace Defense Command (NORAD). Homeland defense and homeland security are top priorities for the governments of Canada and the United States. The Navy will work with the Royal Canadian Navy to ensure common Arctic Region interests are addressed in a complementary manner. The Navy will continue to support NORAD's missions for aerospace warning and control, and maritime warning for threats against the United States and Canada. This unique and enduring partnership between the United States and Canada in defense cooperation is important to our mutual security interests in the Arctic Region.

The Navy and Coast Guard have a decades-long history of cooperation and collaboration. The two services have worked together in close partnership during times of war and peace to protect our Nation's ports and waterways and to promote our maritime security interests overseas. The history of this collaboration between the two sea services acknowledges the distinctive missions, competencies, and cultures of each service. The combined efforts of the Navy and the Coast Guard in the Arctic Ocean will reflect this historic relationship. The Coast Guard and Navy are committed to ensuring safe, secure, and environmentally responsible maritime activity in Arctic Ocean waters and to promoting our other national interests in the Region.

The Arctic Region's vast mineral resources hold significant wealth potential if feasible and cost-effective means can be employed for extraction and transportation to markets.[9] America's continental shelf holds significant energy and mineral resources. Estimates for the economic potential of hydrocarbon resources alone exceed $1 trillion in the U.S. Arctic.[10] The Alaskan Arctic may hold the second largest oil and gas reserves in the Arctic Ocean (after the West Siberian Basin), containing an estimated 29.9 billion barrels of oil, over 221 trillion cubic feet of natural gas, and 5.9 billion barrels of natural gas liquids.[11] In the near-term, mineral resources, particularly rare earth and strategic minerals, iron ore, zinc, nickel, coal, graphite, palladium, and many others will be more important economic drivers in the Arctic Region.

As the Arctic Region becomes increasingly accessible, multinational corporations will likely view exploration of these untapped resources as attractive commercial opportunities for long-term investments. However, the financial, technical, and environmental risks of operating in the Arctic Region create substantial challenges for future production in the region. Whether the resources developed are mineral or hydrocarbon, they must find their way to receptive markets via shipping routes or pipelines. After discovery, oil and gas production in the Arctic Region faces high capital and operating costs. The cost of building infrastructure requires companies to carefully consider whether production volumes and overhead will be commercially feasible to make these investments worthwhile.

Given these current and projected developments, the Navy's existing Arctic Region posture remains appropriate to address the near-term defense requirements of the United States in the Arctic region. During the timeframes assessed for this Roadmap, performance of most national defense missions that entail naval presence in the Arctic Ocean will likely be limited to those summer months when the sea ice is near its minimum, and regional activity is at a peak. Exceptions to the seasonal variation in mission requirements are homeland defense missions. These missions require persistent domain awareness and episodic presence to influence potential adversaries and protect the United States from a range of possible threats.

The Navy's submarine fleet has decades of experience performing missions and exercises under the sea ice. On the other hand, the Navy's surface and air forces have limited operational experience in the region. The Navy will need to periodically evaluate preparedness for operations and conduct training exercises in harsh conditions as changes occur over time in order to ensure the Navy can operate in a more accessible Arctic Ocean.

Regardless of the degree of accessibility, the Arctic Region will remain a unique and harsh operating environment. Naval operations in the Arctic Ocean, outside the Barents, Bering, and Norwegian Seas, require special training, extreme cold-weather modifications for systems and equipment, and complex logistics support. Given the vast distances and virtually no supporting infrastructure, naval forces without specialized equipment and operational experience face substantial impediments. In areas that are seasonally free of ice, the ability of commercial and military vessels to maneuver will remain significantly hindered due to unpredictable locations and movement of ice formations as well as the inadequate and incomplete nautical charting and aids to navigation in many portions of the Arctic Ocean.[12]

Anticipating the impacts of climate change, the Navy will take deliberate steps to prepare for near-term (2014-2020), mid-term (2020-2030), and far-term (beyond 2030) Arctic Ocean operations. As security conditions change and the Arctic Region becomes more accessible, the Navy will re-evaluate its preparedness. The Navy must make targeted investments in Arctic capabilities to hedge against uncertainty and safeguard enduring national interests.

Figure 2: On April 19, 2004, the Los Angeles class attack submarine USS Hampton (SSN-767) surfaced at the geographic North Pole. (United States Navy photo)

1. Purpose

The intent of this Roadmap is to ensure United States Navy forces are prepared to operate in the Arctic Region to promote stability and protect national interests when needed. It provides the Navy's revised strategic guidance for the Arctic Region, as well as an implementation plan tempered by fiscal and operational realities. Additionally, this Roadmap carries forward certain specified tasks from the 2009 Roadmap and completed tasks requiring periodic review.

2. Policy Guidance and United States National Interests in the Arctic

Since publication of the Navy's Arctic Roadmap in 2009, several strategic guidance documents have been revised and new guidance has been released. This update to the Arctic Roadmap builds on the findings of these documents. The Navy's Roadmap for the Arctic Region is derived from the May 2013 *National Strategy for the Arctic Region* and its Implementation Plan (January 2014) and the November 2013 *Department of Defense Arctic Strategy*. The Roadmap is further guided by the January 2012 *Defense Strategic Guidance: Sustaining the U.S. Global Leadership: Priorities for 21*st *Century Defense;* July 2010 *Executive Order 13547: Stewardship of the Ocean, Our Coasts, and the Great Lakes (National Ocean Policy);* the May 2010 *National Security Strategy;* the February 2010 *Quadrennial Defense Review;* January 2009 National Security Presidential Directive – 66/Homeland Security Presidential Directive – 25: *Arctic Region Policy;* the October 2007 *Cooperative Strategy for 21*st *Century Seapower 2007;* and other applicable directives and policies.

The *2010 National Security Strategy* identifies two enduring national interests in the Arctic Region that are relevant to the Navy:
- The security of the United States, its citizens, allies and partners; and
- An international order advanced by United States' leadership that promotes peace, security, and opportunity through stronger cooperation to meet global challenges.

The *2013 National Strategy for the Arctic Region* identifies two lines of effort relevant to the Navy:
- Advance United States' security interests; and
- Strengthen international cooperation.

In November 2013, the Secretary of Defense published the *Department of Defense Arctic Strategy*, identifying two supporting objectives to the National Strategy:
- Ensure security, support safety, and promote defense cooperation; and
- Prepare for a wide range of challenges and contingencies.

In addition to these objectives, the Department of Defense strategy identifies the following actions it will pursue to accomplish these objectives:
- Exercise sovereignty and protect the homeland;
- Engage public and private sector partners to improve domain awareness in the Arctic Region;
- Preserve freedom of the seas in the Arctic Ocean;

- Evolve Arctic Region infrastructure and capabilities consistent with changing conditions;
- Support existing agreements with allies and partners while pursuing new ones to build confidence with key Regional partners;
- Provide support to civil authorities, as directed;
- Partner with other departments and agencies and nations to support human and environmental safety; and
- Support the development of the Arctic Council and other international institutions that promote regional cooperation and the rule of law.

The overarching national security objective is a safe, stable, and secure Arctic Region where the national interests of the United States are advanced and the homeland is protected. The Navy requires Arctic Ocean access to support and protect national interests in the Arctic Region, either independently or in conjunction with other U.S. agencies and partner nations.

3. The Evolving Arctic Region Security Environment

Three primary strategic drivers will determine the extent and timing of potential maritime and naval activity in the Arctic region: (1) *Environmental Conditions*, (2) *Economic Interests and Strategic Resources, (3) Geopolitical Dynamics.*[13]

(1) Environmental Conditions

The Arctic is warming faster than the rest of the globe. In the past 100 years, average Arctic temperatures have increased at almost twice the global average rate.[14] Average Northern

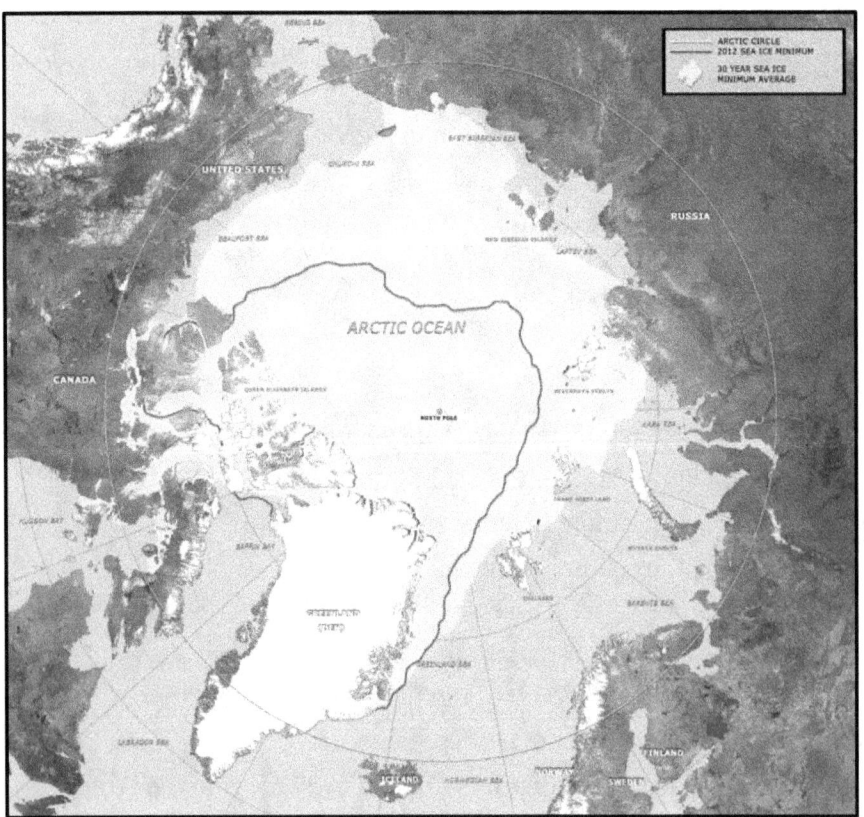

Hemisphere temperatures during the second half of the 20th century were very likely higher than during any other 50-year period in the last 500 years.[15] In 2012, Arctic sea ice reached its smallest extent in recorded history, 1.3 million square miles.[16] The reduction in ice extent has led to an increase in human activity, in resource extraction, fishing, and tourism. Nevertheless, any endeavor in the Arctic Region will have to overcome environmental challenges in the coming

Figure 3: This graphic compares the 30-year sea ice minimum average with the 2012 historical minimum, inside the red line. (United States Navy graphic)

decades as the region warms and the ice continues to recede. With less sea ice cover, the ocean absorbs more heat from the sun during summer, increasing the temperature contrast between the warm ice-free ocean and cold ice surfaces in autumn. This increase in temperature contrast could lead to the development of more frequent and more intense Arctic cyclones. The stronger thermal contrast may also lead to increased likelihood of fog. The impact of reduced sea ice on Arctic weather patterns remains an area of great uncertainty.

To inform this Roadmap update, the Navy assembled a team of Arctic Region subject matter experts from the staffs of the Oceanographer of the Navy; the Chief of Naval Research; Commander, Naval Meteorology and Oceanography Command; Commander, Office of Naval Intelligence; and the President of the Naval Postgraduate School. Advised by additional experts from the National Oceanic and Atmospheric Administration (NOAA), the National Ice Center, the United States Coast Guard, and civilian academia, the team conducted an exhaustive review of current research on Arctic Ocean sea-ice projections in support of naval planning requirements. (A listing of the most influential references is provided in Appendix 1.) This team of experts developed the following consensus assessment, broken into near-, mid-, and far-term time frames:

Near-term: Present to 2020.
Reduction of Arctic Ocean sea ice is expected to continue, and major waterways will become increasingly open. By 2020, the Bering Strait is expected to see open water[17] conditions up to 160 days per year, with 35-45 days of shoulder[18] season. The Northern Sea Route (see Fig. 5) will experience up to 30 days of open water conditions, with up to 45 days of shoulder season conditions. Analysis suggests that the reliable navigability of other routes, including the Transpolar Route and the Northwest Passage, is limited in this timeframe. There will be shoulder season route variability based upon ice age, melt, and movement.

Arctic Sea Route Navigability

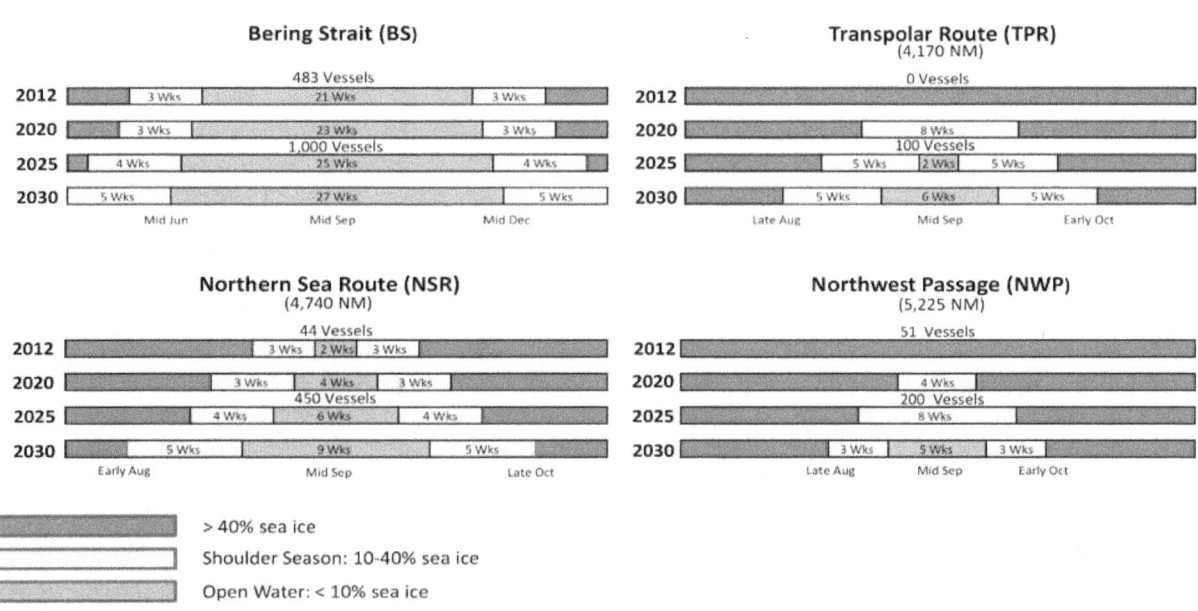

Figure 4: Arctic transit routes availability. Vessel projections courtesy of the Office of Naval Intelligence. (United States Navy graphic)

Mid-term: 2020 to 2030.

This period will see increasing levels of ice melt and increasingly open Arctic Ocean waters. By 2025, the Bering Strait will see up to 175 days of open water (and 50-60 days of shoulder season). These figures increase to 190 days of open water (and up to 70 days of shoulder season) by 2030. For the Northern Sea Route, predictions are for up to 45 days of open water (with 50-60 days of shoulder season) by 2025, increasing to 50-60 days of open water by 2030 (with up to 35 days of shoulder season conditions). This period will begin to see greater accessibility of the Transpolar Route, which is forecast to be open for up to 45 days annually, with 60-70 days of shoulder season. Analysis suggests the reliable navigability of the Northwest Passage will continue to remain limited in this timeframe.

Far-term: Beyond 2030.

In the far-term, environmental conditions are expected to support even greater and more reliable maritime presence in the region. Major waterways are predicted to be consistently open, with a significant increase in traffic over the summer months. The Northern Sea Route and Transpolar Route should be navigable 130 days per year, with open water passage up to 75 days per year. The Northwest Passage will be increasingly open during the late summer and early fall.

(2) Economic Interests and Strategic Resources

The Arctic Region has regained importance since the end of the Cold War, as the retreat of sea ice allows for the potential extraction of resources. The United States Geological Survey estimates undiscovered conventional oil and gas resources at approximately 90 billion barrels of oil, 1,669 trillion cubic feet of natural gas, and 44 billion barrels of natural gas liquids.[19] These deposits equate to about 30 percent of the world's undiscovered natural gas resources, 13 percent of the world's undiscovered oil resources, and 20 percent of the world's liquid natural gas resources. In total, approximately 22 percent of the world's undiscovered hydrocarbon reserves could potentially be found in the Arctic Region.[20] In time, the Northern Sea Route, Transpolar Route, and Northwest Passage will offer shorter transit routes between ports in the Pacific and Atlantic. The 2011 Navy Arctic Mission Analysis stated the following:

Near-term: Present to 2020.

Robust transit shipping will be unlikely in the near-term due to harsh weather, high sea states, and economy-of-scale limitations.[21] Destination shipping in the region along the Northern Sea Route is likely to increase, especially in the Chukchi Sea and the waters off of eastern Russia and Norway, where oil, gas, and mineral exploration, tourism, and fishing appear most viable. Fishing in the United States' exclusive economic zone (EEZ) will remain under a moratorium while the effects of climate change on fish stocks are examined.[22] Exploitation of energy and mineral resources in the Arctic will remain in the exploratory stages.

Mid-term: 2020 to 2030.

The challenges of transit shipping through the Arctic Ocean, such as schedule unpredictability due to weather, sub-seasonal route variability, and economy-of-scale limitations, will continue to limit commercial interest. Though maritime commerce is expected to grow as passage through the Northern Sea Route and Transpolar Route becomes more reliable, the total shipping volume will remain small (less than 2 percent of global maritime traffic).[23] Tourism, to include cruise ship traffic, will continue to increase in the region as accessibility grows. The level of activity in oil, gas, and mining exploration and extraction will depend on global supply and demand and will be tempered by the cost and risk associated with developing proven reserves. Advances from exploration will create demand for robust infrastructure and services along key routes to field development and production. Non-Arctic Region nations will become more present in the Region, particularly to fish, as fishing stocks expand their northern migratory reaches.

Far-term: Beyond 2030.

The exploitation of oil, gas, and mineral resources is expected to continue, resulting in additional maritime traffic to the region as production and transportation models are established and sustained. Fishing in the Region will continue to rise, requiring the United States and other Arctic Region nations to monitor and regulate this activity to ensure sustainable levels of harvesting. The growing economic environment and increased amount of international community activity will require updated international regulations.

The importance of this Region, especially in regard to strategic resources for the United States, could be significant. The projected strategic value of the oil, gas, and other natural resources likely to be found in the Alaskan Arctic indicates that the United States may be eligible to claim one of the largest and richest extended continental shelf sectors in the world, measuring two to three times the size of California.[24] The mean estimated undiscovered, technically-recoverable crude oil off of the Alaskan Arctic is 30 billion barrels which equates to one-third of total Arctic Ocean crude oil resources.[25]

(3) Geopolitical Dynamics

Since the end of the Cold War, the military threat environment in the Arctic Region has diminished significantly and the risk of armed conflict in the Arctic Region is projected to remain low for the foreseeable future.[26] As opposed to combat-related missions, Navy forces are far more likely to be employed in the Arctic Region in support of Coast Guard search and rescue, disaster relief, law enforcement, and other civil emergency/civil support operations.[27] There is a willingness among Arctic Region nations to manage differences through established international mechanisms. The Arctic Council consists of representatives from the eight Arctic nations: Canada, Denmark (representing Greenland and the Faroe Islands), Finland, Iceland, Norway, Sweden, the Russian Federation, and the United States. It serves as a useful forum for promoting cooperation, coordination, and interaction. Arctic nations have a strong economic incentive to preserve this historically stable, non-contentious environment for commercial development. Though the United States has not acceded to the United Nations Convention on the Law of the Sea (UNCLOS), the United States has long considered its provisions related to traditional ocean uses as reflecting customary international law. It serves as the legal framework for important rights and obligations in the Arctic Ocean including the delineation of the outer limits of the continental shelf, protection of the marine environment, freedom of navigation, military survey, and marine scientific research for the region.

In May 2008, the states bordering the Arctic Ocean (the United States, Canada, Greenland, Norway, and the Russian Federation) signed the *Ilulissat Declaration* which concluded that the Convention was the appropriate legal framework for international cooperation and peaceful resolution of maritime disputes in the Arctic.[28] In May 2011, the Arctic Council signed the *Arctic Search and Rescue Agreement*[29] and in May 2013, the Council states signed an *Agreement on Cooperation on Marine Oil Pollution Preparedness and Response in the Arctic*,[30] demonstrating cooperative behavior to improve safety and environmental procedures in the Arctic Ocean. Moreover, the number of nations and other organizations requesting observer status on the Arctic Council is increasing, showing a growing international interest in the Region and the expanding importance of the Arctic Council.

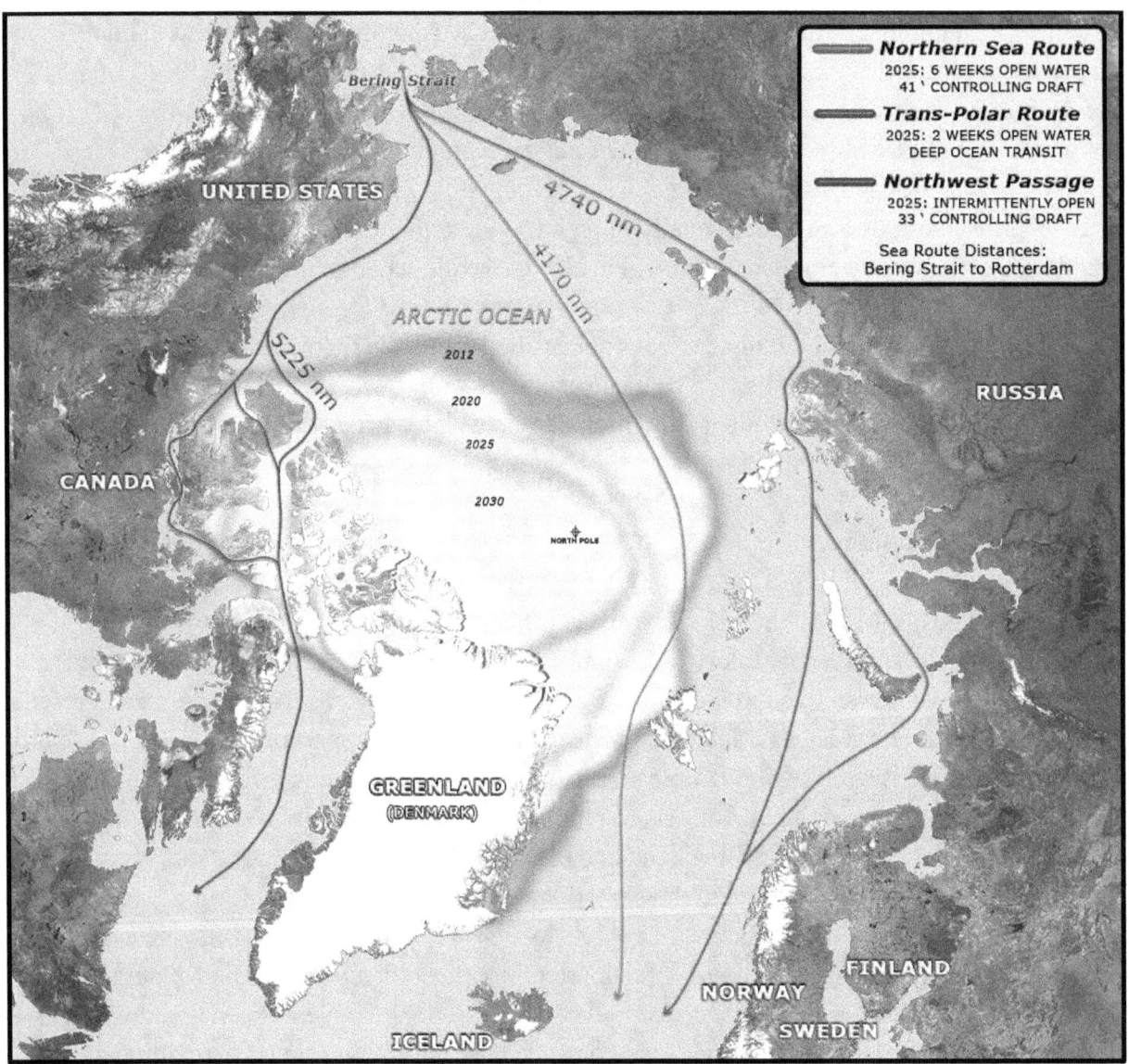

Figure 5: Anticipated future Arctic transit routes superimposed over Navy consensus assessment of sea ice extent minima. (United States Navy graphic)

It remains unlikely that any of the five Arctic littoral states will risk a large-scale, intrastate military conflict. There remains a possibility that tensions could increase due to misperceptions, and rhetoric, as well as the unforeseen dynamics of economic interests in the region.[31] Excessive extended continental shelf claims made by Arctic nations to the Commission on the Limits of the Continental Shelf (CLCS) may cause tension and create political uncertainty. Given the resource wealth that could be at stake, a resulting standoff could indeed lead to disputes and military posturing by rival nations. Non-Arctic nations may consider staking a claim to areas outside the resource claims of the Arctic nations, particularly those in the central Arctic Ocean, without acknowledging their obligations under UNCLOS and rejecting the legal control of the areas by the International Seabed Authority (ISA). Another possible source of pressure could come from the migration of fish to previously unreachable fishing grounds where ownership is unclear from one nation's exclusive economic zone to that of another. A combination of these factors contributes to a possibility of localized episodes of friction in the Arctic Region, despite the peaceful intentions of the Arctic nations.

4. United States Navy Strategic Objectives for the Arctic Region

Based on the drivers, trends, and predictions noted above, and in alignment with higher level guidance, the Navy strategic objectives for the Arctic Region are:

- *Ensure United States Arctic sovereignty and provide homeland defense;*
- *Provide ready naval forces* to respond to crisis and contingencies;
- *Preserve freedom of the seas*; and
- *Promote partnerships* within the United States Government and with international allies.

Ensure United States Arctic sovereignty and provide homeland defense. A primary Navy responsibility is to protect the homeland, its citizens, and critical infrastructure. The changing environment may create new opportunities and security challenges in the "high north." The Navy will protect American sovereign rights and jurisdiction through flexible, periodic presence, and contribute to homeland defense in conjunction with the Joint Force. The Navy will ensure it remains prepared to operate in the Arctic Region to counter any threats to the homeland that may arise.

Figure 6: In 2007, the guided missile cruiser USS Normandy (CG-60) approached an ice field in waters north of Iceland. (United States Navy photo)

Provide ready naval forces to respond to crisis and contingencies. Environmental information, safety at sea and in the air, communication and data challenges, infrastructure, and regional expertise are some, but not all, of the current gaps and seams that must be overcome to operate in the Arctic Region. The Navy's Arctic Roadmap identifies the capabilities required to operate in Arctic conditions and develops the plan to overcome these gaps and seams. The Navy will further develop doctrine, operating procedures, and tactics, techniques, and procedures to specifically guide operations in the Arctic environment. The

15

Roadmap directs review and identification of requirements for improvements to platforms, sensors, and weapons systems that facilitate sustained, safe operations in the Region. This includes cold-weather training, a better communications architecture, and logistical support. The geography and climate of the Arctic Region will pose challenges to naval logistics. The Navy must examine the role and limitations of operational energy access including: how fuel will be distributed to the Region, to air and surface platforms, and how naval personnel deployed to the Region will be trained in energy conservation and environmentally sustainable practices. An increased knowledge of the physical environment will help the Navy better predict ice conditions, shifting navigable waterways, and weather patterns to aid in safe navigation and operations at sea. The Navy will grow Arctic expertise and experience through increased research and information sharing among our allies and partners. Finally, improvement in operational readiness through education, knowledge, training, and research will allow the Navy to provide a quick response to Arctic Region contingency operations.

Preserve freedom of the seas. Access to the global commons and freedom of the seas are a national priority. The Navy will support access for the safe, secure, and free flow of resources and commerce in the Region. Strategic resources and trade routes will be a primary driver for Arctic and non-Arctic nations alike to seek economic prosperity. The Navy will contribute to stability and security as economic activity increases.

Promote partnerships within the United States Government and with international allies in support of security and safety. The Arctic Region poses unique operational challenges beyond the weather to include communications and navigational hazards. These challenges provide opportunities to cooperate with interagency partners and international allies, sharing limited resources to improve situational awareness and develop a Common Maritime Picture (CMP) of the Arctic Ocean. In conjunction with interagency and international partners, the Navy will seek to improve Maritime Domain Awareness (MDA), information sharing, and communications. Currently, Arctic MDA is assessed as adequate. However, as traffic and Regional activity rise in the coming decades, the Navy will seek to improve overall MDA capability. To build the ties of trust and confidence that underpin strong alliances and partnerships, it is essential to operate and train together. Multilateral training, operations, and exercises in the Arctic Ocean such as NORTHERN EAGLE[32] and NANOOK[33] will improve knowledge of the Region and provide a positive foundation for future missions.

5. United States Navy Leadership Role and Missions in the Arctic Region

The Navy will continue to have a significant leadership role in the Arctic Region to enable the joint and interagency community to operate in this hard-to-reach, isolated, and harsh environment. Through its global reach capability and worldwide command and control, Navy leadership will support joint and interagency efforts, enhance information sharing, and develop enterprise solutions that can be employed across United States Government and allied partner agencies operating in the Region.

To improve MDA, weather and ocean prediction, and safety of navigation, the Navy will continue to work closely with the National Geospatial-Intelligence Agency (NGA), NOAA, the

Department of Homeland Security (DHS), other interagency partners, as well as Arctic and non-Arctic nations. As the Department of Defense Executive Agent for MDA, the Navy plays a lead role in interagency and international efforts to share maritime information. Additionally, Navy has Title 10 responsibilities to "maximize the safety and effectiveness of maritime vessels, aircraft, and forces of the armed forces" [34] by means of marine data collection, numerical weather and ocean prediction, and forecasting of hazardous weather and ocean conditions. The Navy may extend similar support to coalition forces that are operating with United States' forces. Title 10 also charges the Navy to collect, process, and provide hydrographic information to NGA to support preparation of maps, charts, books, and geodetic products by that agency.

The Navy executes several key missions in concert with joint forces, interagency stakeholders, and allies and partners, to protect sovereignty, ensure freedom of the seas, and defend the homeland in order to maintain stability and prevent conflict in the Arctic Region. The Navy will maintain the capability to influence adversaries with a skilled force that is trained and equipped to operate in the Arctic environment. The key functions and missions the Navy will lead or support in the coming decades are:

Maritime Security. Arctic nations are aligned in their support for enhanced safety and security in the Arctic Region. The Navy will continue to operate in the Arctic Region and be ready to conduct maritime patrol and maritime interception operations, and support Coast Guard operations as required.

Sea Control.[35] The Navy has a global responsibility to protect vital sea lanes and operating areas, including defending the Nation's maritime borders and EEZs. The geostrategic importance of the Bering Strait will increase as resource extraction, shipping, fishing, and tourism increases. The Navy will be forward deployed and prepared to protect United States' maritime access and interests as the Arctic Ocean sea lanes begin to open.

Power Projection.[36] Naval forces provide a flexible and versatile option to ensure national interests are protected. The Navy's unique capabilities allow it to rapidly and effectively deploy and sustain forces in and from multiple dispersed locations to respond to crises, contribute to deterrence, and to enhance regional stability.

Freedom of Navigation. United States' policy since 1983 provides that the United States will exercise and assert its navigation and overflight rights and freedoms on a worldwide basis in a manner that is consistent with customary international law. The Navy will guarantee freedom of navigation in Arctic Ocean waters and help ensure the free flow of commerce on the global commons.

Search and Rescue (SAR). The extreme distances, limited infrastructure, and assets make SAR challenging in the Arctic Region. The Navy will provide support as required to search and rescue missions conducted and led by the Coast Guard and as directed in support of international partners.

Disaster Response/Defense Support of Civil Authorities (DSCA). The movement of resources through the air or on the sea across great distances by naval forces trained and equipped to support other United States Government agencies in the Arctic Region may be required. The Arctic environment, combined with increasing maritime traffic and energy exploration, may increase the probability of a maritime or environmental disaster occurring in the mid-to-long term. The Navy will remain ready to support critical and likely missions such as pollution response and SAR; integrated planning efforts with local, state, federal, and native communities; strengthen interoperability with the Coast Guard and international partners; and develop processes, procedures, joint training, and exercises to gain operational proficiency.

6. United States Navy Ways and Means for Near-Term, Mid-Term, and Far-Term Operations

Near-term: Present to 2020.

The Navy will continue to provide capability and presence primarily through undersea and air assets. Surface ship operations will be limited to open water operations in the near-term. Even in open water conditions, weather factors, including sea ice, must be considered in operational risk assessments. During shoulder seasons, the Navy may employ ice strengthened Military Sealift Command (MSC) ships to conduct Navy missions.

By 2020, the Navy will increase the number of personnel trained in Arctic operations. The Navy will grow expertise in all domains by continuing to participate in exercises, scientific missions, and personnel exchanges in Arctic-like conditions. Personnel exchanges will provide Sailors with opportunities to learn best practices from other United States' military services, interagency partners, and international allies and partners.

The Navy will refine or develop the necessary strategy, policy, plans, and requirements for the Arctic Region. Additionally, the Navy will continue to study and make informed decisions on pursuing investments to better facilitate Arctic operations. The Navy will emphasize low cost, long-lead time activities to match capability and capacity to future demands. The Navy will update operating requirements and procedures for personnel, ships, and aircraft to operate in the Region with interagency partners and allies. Through ongoing exercises, such as Ice Exercise (ICEX) and Scientific Ice Expeditions (SCICEX)[37] research, and transits through the region by Navy submarines, aircraft and surface vessels, the Navy will continue to learn more about the evolving operating environment. The Navy will focus on areas where it provides unique capabilities and will leverage joint and coalition partners to fill identified gaps and seams.

Mid-term: 2020 to 2030.

By 2030, the Navy will have the necessary training and personnel to respond to contingencies and emergencies affecting national security. As the Arctic Ocean becomes increasingly ice-free, surface vessels will operate in the expanding open water areas. The Navy will improve its capabilities by participating in increasingly complex exercises and training with regional partners. While primary risks in the mid-term will likely be meeting search and rescue or disaster response mission demands, the Navy may also be called upon to ensure freedom of navigation in Arctic Ocean waters.[38] The Navy will work to mitigate the gaps and seams and transition its

Arctic Ocean operations from a capability to provide periodic presence to a capability to operate deliberately for sustained periods when needed.

Far-term: Beyond 2030.
In the far-term, Navy will be capable of supporting sustained operations in the Arctic Region as needed to meet national policy guidance. The Navy will provide trained and equipped personnel, along with surface, subsurface, and air capabilities, to achieve Combatant Commander's objectives. The high confidence of diminished ice coverage and navigable waterways for much of the year will enable naval forces to operate forward, ready to respond to any potential threat to national security, or to provide contingency response. Far-term risks include increased potential for search and rescue and DSCA, but may also require naval forces to have a greater focus on maritime security and freedom of navigation in the Region.

7. Roadmap Execution
Appendix 2 identifies completed actions of the 2009 Roadmap. Appendix 3 provides updated actions for the implementation of the 2014-2030 Roadmap. The action items are assigned to responsible Navy offices according to the doctrine, organization, training, materiel, leadership and education, and personnel and facilities (DOTMLPF-P) process with suspense dates for completion. Supporting organizations are identified but are not limited to those listed. Lastly, metrics will be developed for tracking and periodic reports will be provided to the Chief of Naval Operations (CNO).

8. Conclusion
The Arctic Region, with its vast expanse, severe climate, and rich natural resources, is a challenge and an opportunity for the Navy. Naval security and international naval cooperation have always been critical components of United States' Arctic policy. As the Arctic Ocean opens, these components will increase as activity rises. This Navy Arctic Roadmap update underscores the need to develop strong cooperative partnerships with interagency and international Arctic Region stakeholders. It acknowledges the role climate change plays in energy security, research and science, the economy, fisheries, tourism, the assertion of sovereignty, and other related issues. To be prepared to address the emerging challenges caused by the opening of the Arctic Ocean waters, this Roadmap recognizes that changes in the environment must be continuously examined and taken into account. The Navy will take deliberate steps to anticipate and prepare for Arctic Region operations in the near-term (2014-2020), mid-term (2020-2030), and far-term (beyond 2030). The key will be to balance potential investments with other Service priorities.

Appendix 1

Primary References Used to Inform the Arctic Sea Ice and Sea Lane Predictions

Humpert, M., and A. Raspotnik. "The Future of Arctic Shipping Along the Transpolar Sea Route." *Arctic Yearbook* (2012): 281-307.

Maslowski, W., J. Clement Kinney, M. Higgins, and A. Roberts. "The Future of Arctic Sea Ice." *Annual Review of Earth and Planetary Sciences* 40 (2012): 625¬654.

Massonnet, F., T. Fichefet, H. Goosse, C. Bitz, G. Philippon-Berthier, M. Holland, and P.Y. Barriat. "Constraining Projections of Summer Arctic Sea Ice." *The Cryosphere Discuss* 6 (2012): 2931¬2959.

Overland, J. E., and M. Wang. "When Will the Summer Arctic be Nearly Sea Ice Free?" *Geophysical Research Letters*, Volume 40, Issue 10 (20 May 2013): 2097–2101.

Smith, L.C. and S.R. Stephenson. "New Trans-Arctic Shipping Routes Navigable by Midcentury." *Proceedings of the National Academy of Sciences* Vol 110 No 13 (2013).

Sou, T. and G. Flato. "Sea Ice in the Canadian Arctic Archipelago: Modeling the Past (1950–2004) and the Future (2041–60)." *Journal of Climate* 22 (2009): 2181–2198.

U.S. Navy. "U.S. Navy Arctic Mission Analysis." Washington, DC (2011).

Markus, T., J. C. Stroeve and J. Miller. "Recent Changes in Arctic Sea Ice melt onset, freeze up, and melt season length." *Journal of Geophysical Research* 114, C12024 (2009).

Wang, M., and J. Overland. "Projected Future Duration of the Sea-ice-free Season in the Alaskan Arctic." *Progress in Oceanography*. [Forthcoming]

Appendix 2

2009 Roadmap Completed Actions

- Analysis of the Strategic Environment
- Arctic Mission Analysis
- Increased participation in discussions with the U.S. Coast Guard and Arctic Nation Navies
- Formalized strategic objectives for the Arctic
- Articulated Unified Command Plan (UCP) position for the Arctic, and the Arctic features prominently in the Navy Strategic Plan
- Assessed Fleet Arctic Readiness
- Increased operations in the Arctic:
    - In 2009, the Navy deployed the aircraft carrier JOHN C. STENNIS north of the Arctic Circle.
    - In 2010, the Navy deployed USS PORTER north of the Arctic Circle in support of exercise NANOOK 2010.
    - In 2011, the Navy brought USS NEW HAMPSHIRE and USS CONNECTICUT to an organized science exercise (SCICEX) beneath an ice station.
    - In 2012, the cruiser USS LAKE ERIE and destroyer USS DECATUR operated north of the Arctic Circle.
    - In 2012, the destroyer USS FARRAGUT operated in the Barents Sea in support of NORTHERN EAGLE, a combined Russian-U.S.-Norwegian exercise.
    - In 2012, Naval Undersea Warfare Center and NASA operated Unmanned Undersea Vehicles (UUVs) to image icebergs along east coast of Greenland.
    - During odd-numbered years, Navy participates in the joint Northern Edge exercise in the Gulf of Alaska.

- GLOBAL SHIPPING GAME at NWC in 2010
- FLEET ARCTIC OPERATIONS GAME at NWC in 2011
- Arctic Capability Based Assessment (CBA)
- Included Arctic requirements in Navy Sponsor Program Proposals for POM-14
- Development and implementation of Strategic Outreach and Strategic Communications plans
- Arctic Environmental Observation and Prediction CBA
- Continuation of the SCICEX program
- Contributed to development of the National Ocean Policy for the Arctic
- ONR established a new "Arctic and Global Prediction" Program to address Arctic S&T needs identified by the Navy, addressing basic research in Arctic physical sciences, technology development, and prediction capability development at multiple lead times.

Appendix 3

Arctic Roadmap Implementation Plan

1.1 Strategy, Policy, Missions and Plans

Actions	Lead	Support	DOTMLPF	Suspense
1.1.1: Establish a working group to codify near-term and potential mid-term requirements to inform POM-16 guidance and annually thereafter.	OPNAV N9	OPNAV N1 OPNAV N2/N6 OPNAV N3/N5 OPNAV N4 OPNAV N9 EUCOM NORTHCOM USFFC/CPF	D	Q1, FY14
1.1.2: Identify metrics suitable for CNO progress reports on Section 1.1 (Strategy, Policy, Missions, and Plans) of Arctic Roadmap.	OPNAV N3/N5	Director TFCC TFCC	D	Q3, FY14
1.1.3: Advocate that OSD designate SECNAV as the Department of Defense (DOD) Executive Agent for the Arctic.	OPNAV N3/N5		D	Q3, FY14
1.1.4: Reflect the Arctic objectives in Guidance for Employment of the Force (GEF).	OPNAV N3/N5	OPNAV N2/N6 OPNAV N4 OPNAV N8 OPNAV N9 USFFC/CPF ONR	D	Q3, FY14
1.1.5: Incorporate specific required Navy Arctic capabilities in the Classified Annex to CS-21R.	OPNAV N3/N5		D	Q3, FY14
1.1.6: Incorporate the Classified Annex to CS-21R guidance relating to Arctic capabilities in Sponsor Program Proposals for POM-16 and annually thereafter.	Resource Sponsors	OPNAV N2/N6 OPNAV N4 OPNAV N8 OPNAV N9 USFFC ONR	D	Q3, FY14 (FY14-20)
1.1.7: Conduct Arctic intelligence and front-end security assessment and provide report to CNO to inform POM-16 and annually thereafter. • Characterize current and predicted threats to the Arctic region in 2020, 2030, and 2040. Focus on threats to U.S. national security, although threats to maritime safety and security, as well as energy security and resilience will be considered. • Assess range of potential environmental conditions • For range of conditions that might occur, assess how access and activities in the Arctic might evolve • How this impacts national/maritime safety and security and implications for USN/USCG (and joint & coalition) capability/capacity • Compare the projected time for Arctic environmental and activity changes with the time needed to develop required capabilities • Consider interdependencies between actors and actions in the Arctic and how incentives and decisions are influenced by other actors' decisions.	OPNAV N2/N6	OPNAV N3/N5 OPNAV N4 OPNAV N9 CNE USFFC CPF NWC NPS OJAG ONI ONR USCG USNA	D	Q3, FY14
1.1.8: Develop Arctic engagement plan focusing on partnerships with international, interagency and private sector stakeholders that enhance Arctic security.	OPNAV N3/N5	DUSN PPOI	D, O	Q3, FY14

1.1.9: Incorporate Arctic engagements in Navy Campaign Support Plan.	OPNAV N3/N5	OPNAV N2/N6 OPNAV N4 OPNAV N8 OPNAV N9 USFFC/CPF NWDC OJAG ONR	D		Q4, FY14
1.1.10: Ensure adequate environmental compliance (Marine Mammal Protection Act, Endangered Species Act, National Environmental Policy Act and Executive Order 12114) for at-sea training and testing activities in the Arctic regions. • Prepare Arctic compliance strategy and include in POM 16 submittal. • Gather training and testing activities requirements to determine environmental coverage needs • Initiate and execute planning and compliance documentation pending OPNAV resource sponsor funding.	USFFC	OPNAV N3/N5 OPNAV N4 ONR NAVAIR NAVSEA	D		 Q1, FY14 Q1, FY15 Q2, FY16
1.1.11: Continue to advocate for U.S. accession to the United Nations Convention on the Law of the Sea (UNCLOS) as determined by Department of State (taking into account Senate reception). As required, provide strategy, policy and operational support for U.S. accession to UNCLOS as applicable to Navy's interests in the Arctic. • Talking points, information papers, or briefings for senior Navy leadership as requested. • Continue to participate in any/all interagency working groups in support of U.S. accession efforts.	OJAG	OPNAV N3/N5 CHINFO OLA	D		Ongoing

2.0 Operate Safely and Proficiently in the Arctic

2.1 Operations and Training

Actions	Lead	Support	DOTMLPF	Suspense
2.1.1: Identify metrics suitable for CNO progress reports on Section 2.1 (Operations and Training) of Arctic Roadmap.	USFFC	Director TFCC TFCC	D	Q3, FY14
2.1.2: Continue submarine inter-fleet transfers through Arctic.	USFFC/CPF	OPNAV N3/N5 ASL C6F COMSUBFOR MSC	T	FY14-20
2.1.3: Direct TYCOMs to update Fleet guidance on Arctic operations to include: • Planned operations in the Arctic to begin defining requirements and refining capability gaps • Operational risk management model that properly identifies the risks associated with operating in the Arctic based on current capabilities and observed weather conditions • Assessment of Fleet doctrine for adequacy	USFFC/CPF	OPNAV N3/N5 MSC	D, O, T, M, L	Q1, FY15
2.1.4: Develop personnel exchange program with regional partners.	OPNAV N1	OPNAV N3/N5 C6F MSC USFFC/CPF USCG	T, L, P	Q1, FY15
2.1.5: Determine adequacy of Navy supply system to support unit deployments to the Arctic region. • Upon requirements determination by USFFC, ensure a baseline inventory of material is available and address significant deficiencies that could compromise energy and material resiliency, placing units at risk for near-term Arctic operations.	OPNAV N4 NAVSUP	MSC TYCOMS USFFC NAVAIR NAVSEA DLA USCG USMC	M	Q1, FY15
2.1.6: Update U.S. Navy Cold Weather Handbook for Surface Ships (1988).	OPNAV N9	USFFC/CPF NWDC	D, O, T	Q1, FY15
2.1.7: Direct TYCOMs to generate guidance and training requirements. Guidance shall: • Evaluate Arctic training capabilities • Address significant deficiencies that increase risk for near-term Arctic operations • Include Arctic material in training curriculums to improve the Fleet's understanding of the Arctic	USFFC/CPF	OPNAV N1 OPNAV N3/N5 OPNAV N8 OPNAV N9 CPF TYCOMS NETC NPS NWC NWDC USNA	D, T, L	Q1, FY15 Q2, FY15 Q2, FY15
2.1.8: Identify requirements to establish Arctic Center of Excellence.	OPNAV N2/N6	NPS NWC ONI ONR USNA	T	Q4, FY15

2.1.9: Develop a long range exercise and training plan that prioritizes and increases participation/visibility in scheduled Arctic exercises, such as: • Arctic Edge (Bi-Annual) • Arctic Shield (Annual) • BALTOPS (Annual) • Cold Response (Annual) • FRUKUS (Annual) • ICEX (Tri-Annual) • Northern Challenge (Annual) • Northern Eagle (Bi-Annual) • Northern Edge (Bi-Annual) • Operation NANOOK (Annual) • SAREX (Annual) • Arctic Zephyr (Annual) • For each exercise, provide lessons learned to NWDC for retention and action. • For those exercises identified as priorities, resource participating platforms and personnel. • Annually assess new opportunities for Arctic training.	USFFC	OPNAV N2/N6 OPNAV N3/N5 OPNAV N4 OPNAV N8 OPNAV N9 TFCC C6F COMSUBFOR CPF ASL MSC TYCOMS NAVSEA NWC NWDC USCG	L, T, M	Q1, FY16 (FY16-20)
2.1.10: Develop Arctic CONOPs for Naval platforms and update as new capabilities are developed.	USFFC	OPNAV N3/N5 OPNAV N4 NAVSEA NWDC	D, O, T, M, L, P, F	Q1, FY18
2.1.11: Integrate the testing of sensors and systems into Arctic exercises and ops.	USFFC	OPNAV N3/N5 OPNAV N4 NAVSEA NWDC ONR	D, O, T, M, L, P, F	Q1, FY18

2.2 Science and Technology

Actions	Lead	Support	DOTMLPF	Suspense
2.2.1: Identify metrics suitable for CNO progress reports on Section 2.2 (Science and Technology) of Arctic Roadmap.	ONR	Director TFCC TFCC	D	Q3, FY14
2.2.2: Incorporate Arctic related science and technology (S&T) requirements and emphasize within the Classified Annex to CS-21R. Include cyber and non-kinetic weapon systems.	ONR	OPNAV N2/N6 OPNAV N3/N5 OPNAV N8 TFCC USFFC NAVSEA NWDC	M	Q3, FY14
2.2.3: Establish SCICEX as a priority. When operational requirements permit, SCICEX accommodation missions (SAMs) will be conducted according to the Science Plans agreed to by the SCICEX Science Advisory and Interagency Committees.	OPNAV N9	USFFC CPF COMSUBFOR ASL CNMOC ONR	T, M	FY14-20
2.2.4: Support and improve access to previously classified information to be used by climate research community. Continue, and seek opportunities, to improve U.S. Navy collaboration and cooperative involvement with non-U.S. Navy entities in the Measurements of Earth Data for Environmental Analysis (MEDEA) Program.	OPNAV N2/N6	USFFC CNMOC ASL NIPO ONR	M	Q3, FY15
2.2.5: Provide S&T plans for Arctic Assessment and Prediction to include: • UUV/unmanned aerial vehicle (UAV) performance in the Arctic • Waves and swell in the Arctic • Arctic Ocean circulation and stratification • Acoustic propagation in the Arctic environment • Sea level rise and mass balance of glaciers and ice sheets • Impact of Arctic environment on Naval systems • Development of new technologies and adoption of existing technologies (e.g., sensors, platforms and communications) for sustained operation and observation in the Arctic • Socio-economic and geopolitical issues that might drive future Naval activity in the Arctic	ONR OPNAV N2/N6	OPNAV N8 TFCC USFFC/CPF CNMOC ONI NAVSEA SPAWAR	M	Q4, FY15
2.2.6: Increase ONR's Arctic Research Efforts and brief milestones annually to Chief of Naval Research. Improving the Navy's ability to understand and predict the Arctic physical environment at a variety of time and space scales. • Sea ice extent forecasting and prediction • Ice and snow thickness prediction • Iceberg analysis, lifecycle and dynamics • Seasonal Ice Zone Reconnaissance Surveys • Ice, sea, air interaction physics • Seasonal and sub-seasonal climate prediction forecasts • Improve understanding of the physical environment and processes in the Arctic Ocean.	ONR	OPNAV N2/N6 CNMOC TFCC NPS NWC NWDC USFFC USNA	M	FY16-20

2.3 Environmental Observation and Prediction

Actions	Lead	Support	DOTMLPF	Suspense
2.3.1: Identify metrics suitable for CNO progress reports on Section 2.3 (Environmental Observation and Prediction) of Arctic Roadmap.	OPNAV N2/N6	Director TFCC TFCC	D	Q3, FY14
2.3.2: Develop Arctic environmental observing and prediction engagement plan focusing on cooperative partnerships with international, interagency and private sector stakeholders that enhance Arctic environmental observation and mapping.	OPNAV N2/N6	OPNAV N3/N5 Director TFCC USFFC CNMOC NIPO ONR USCG	D, L, T	Q3, FY14
2.3.3: Produce a holistic Arctic environmental sensing plan (ocean, surface, sub-surface and space based) to close validated gaps. Plan will include: • Focus on acoustic data to support anti-submarine warfare (ASW) operations • Sensing strategy • Implementation and fielding • Use of unmanned systems for Arctic data collection, monitoring, and research	OPNAV N2/N6	Director TFCC USFFC CNMOC ONR USCG	D, O, T, M, P	Q3, FY14 Q3, FY15 FY15-18 FY18
2.3.4: Improve traditional meteorological forecast capability in the polar regions through the following: • Evaluate current capability • Determine improvement areas • Define required investment	USFFC	OPNAV N2/N6 Director TFCC CNMOC ONR	T, M	Q3, FY14 Q4, FY14 Q1, FY15
2.3.5: Encourage research into and development of comprehensive Arctic System Models (ocean-ice-wave-atmosphere) for forecasts at multiple time scales, including activities to quantify and characterize uncertainty in long range climate and ice forecasting capabilities.	ONR	OPNAV N2/N6 TFCC USFFC CNMOC USA CRREL USCG	T, M	Q4, FY14
2.3.6: Ensure Arctic requirements (environmental observation and prediction capabilities) are reflected in Sponsor Program Proposals (SPPs) in alignment with Classified Annex to CS-21R. If required, SPPs will include recommendations relating to the Navy's capability gaps regarding Arctic operations identified in previous CBAs and will include, but not be limited to: • S&T needs • Research and development (R&D) requirements • Leveraging Joint, interagency and international partnerships to find efficiencies and/or economies of scale	OPNAV N2/N6	OPNAV N8 TFCC USFFC NAVSEA ONR	T, M	FY14-15, annually
2.3.7: Establish a cadre of Arctic environmental Observers / Forecasters (Ice, Ocean and Atmospheric) and training pipeline.	OPNAV N2/N6	OPNAV N1 USFFC CNMOC	D, T, P	FY14-20
2.3.8: Sustain development and participation in Earth System Prediction Capability (ESPC): • Develop the capability for coupled ocean-atmosphere-land-cryosphere modeling in the Navy and focused on seasonal-to-decadal timescale prediction to support strategic decisions related to operations, platforms and facilities.	OPNAV N2/N6	Director TFCC USFFC CNMOC ONR	O, M	FY14-20
2.3.9: Develop and execute a CONOPS for Arctic environmental Observer / Forecaster (Ice,	USFFC	OPNAV N2/N6 OPNAV N3/N5	D, O, T	Q3, FY15

Ocean and Atmospheric) support to Navy platforms operating in the Arctic that includes organizational structure and location.		CNMOC NWDC USA CRREL USCG		
2.3.10: Update Forecaster's Handbook for the Arctic, 1989.	USFFC	OPNAV N2/N6 CNMOC NRL ONR USCG	O, T	Q1, FY16
2.3.11: Support efforts to research, develop, resource and sustain an Arctic environmental observation system to support U.S. operations (Surface, Subsurface, HA/DR, SAR, and Air) in the Arctic (interagency effort).	OPNAV N2/N6	OPNAV N8 USFFC CNMOC ONR PEO C4I SPAWAR	M	FY16-20

2.4 Safe Navigation

Actions	Lead	Support	DOTMLPF	Suspense
2.4.1: Identify metrics suitable for CNO progress reports on Section 2.4 (Safe Navigation) of Arctic Roadmap.	OPNAV N2/N6	Director TFCC TFCC	D	Q3, FY14
2.4.2: Initiate an Arctic Nation Navy hydrographic survey data sharing and planning effort.	OPNAV N2/N6	OPNAV N3/N5 TFCC USFFC CNMOC NIPO NOAA USCG	D, L	Q3, FY14
2.4.3: Sustain Arctic Nation Navy hydrographic survey data sharing and planning effort (2.4.2)	OPNAV N2/N6	OPNAV N3/N5 TFCC USFFC CNMOC NIPO NOAA USCG	D, L	FY15-20
2.4.4: Develop multi-year hydrographic/bathymetric survey plan to address prioritized Navy Arctic Basin survey requirements through USFFC Oceanographic, Hydrographic and Bathymetric (OHB) and Fleet Oceanographic Support Workshop (FOSW) process.	USFFC	OPNAV N2/N6 NCCs CNMOC MSC	D, M	Q4, FY14
2.4.5: Ensure Arctic requirements (oceanographic, hydrographic and bathymetric data collection capabilities) are reflected in Sponsor Program Proposals in alignment with Classified Annex to CS-21R.	OPNAV N2/N6	OPNAV N8 USFFC CNMOC	T, M	FY14-20, annually
2.4.6: Continue to foster current and new partnerships (interagency and allied) regarding data exchanges.	OPNAV N2/N6	OPNAV N3/N5 OPNAV N8 TFCC USFFC CNMOC NIPO NOAA	D, L	FY14-20
2.4.7: Leverage USCG, commercial, and partner nation icebreakers for real-world operations and emergencies as required.	USFFC	OPNAV N3/N5 NIPO USCG	D, O	FY14-20
2.4.8: Coordinate with NGA, NOAA and USCG to develop a national hydrographic plan in support of the National Strategy for the Arctic region.	OPNAV N2/N6	OPNAV N3/N5 OPNAV N8 Director TFCC USFFC CNMOC NSF USCG USA CRREL	D, T, M, P	Q1, FY15
2.4.9: Coordinate with USCG to identify safe navigational corridors and NAVAID requirements.	USFFC	OPNAV N2/N6 TFCC CNMOC USCG	O, M	Q4, FY15
2.4.10: Support initiatives of the Commandant of the Coast Guard to define future USCG icebreaker requirements.	Director TFCC	OPNAV N3/N5 OPNAV N2/N6 OPNAV N8 OPNAV N9 NAVSEA USCG	D	FY15-20

2.5 Command, Control, Communications, Computers, Intelligence, Surveillance, and Reconnaissance

Actions	Lead	Support	DOTMLPF	Suspense
2.5.1: Identify metrics suitable for CNO progress reports on Section 2.5 (C4ISR) of Arctic Roadmap.	OPNAV N2/N6	Director TFCC TFCC	D	Q3, FY14
2.5.2: Ensure current and programmed Navy Arctic SATCOM requirements are used in DoD space program development.	OPNAV N2/N6		D, O, T, M, L, P, F	Q2, FY14
2.5.3: Advocate for U.S./Canadian agreement regarding communications and weather Arctic Satellite capability.	OPNAV N2/N6	OPNAV N3/N5 USFFC OJAG	D, O	Q4, FY14
2.5.4: Assess the Classified Annex to CS-21R's guidance, if any, relating to required C4ISR capability in the Arctic, and address these requirements in Sponsor Program Proposals.	OPNAV N2/N6	OPNAV N8 TFCC USFFC	T, M	FY14-20, annually
2.5.5: Establish Arctic ISR requirements for space, manned and unmanned options. • Determine C4ISR interoperability with USCG and USAF	OPNAV N2/N6	OPNAV N8 OPNAV N9 USFFC USCG	D, O, T, M, L, P, F	Q2, FY15
2.5.6: Ensure the ongoing Protected SATCOM Assessment of Alternatives analyze existing and future high data rate communications in the Arctic. • Determine high data rate requirements • Investigate ways to optimize satellite communications in light of ionic disturbances which degrade signals • Optimize orbits of most communications satellite constellations to support military communications in the Arctic • Determine if operational payloads currently in orbit providing continuous satellite coverage above 65°N are sufficient for Navy operations in the Arctic • Extend the data rate to speed the transmission of imagery	OPNAV N2/N6	OPNAV N8 USFFC CNMOC	D, O, T, M, L, P, F	Q3, FY14

2.6 Installations and Facilities

Actions	Lead	Support	DOTMLPF	Suspense
2.6.1: Identify metrics suitable for CNO progress reports on Section 2.6 (Installations and Facilities) of Arctic Roadmap.	OPNAV N4	Director TFCC TFCC		Q3, FY14
2.6.2: Identify requirements to establish Aerial Ports of Debarkation (APODs) and Sea Ports of Debarkation (SPODs) in the Arctic.	OPNAV N4	OPNAV N3/N5 CNIC MSC NAVFAC	O, M, F	Q4, FY14
2.6.3: Confirm existing and planned U.S. and international government or industry infrastructure. • Evaluate capability of existing ports and airfields to support Navy operational requirements	OPNAV N4	OPNAV N3/N5 USFFC N3/N5 CNIC NIPO	O, M, F	Q4, FY14 Q4, FY16
2.6.4: Ensure defined Arctic infrastructure requirements are reflected in Sponsor Program Proposals in alignment with Navy Strategic Plan and Classified Annex to CS-21R. (Review annually in context of changing climate.) • Identify/develop Arctic installations, airfields and hanger requirements • Conduct environmental impact assessments to assure environmental compliance	OPNAV N4	OPNAV N2/N6 OPNAV N3/N5 OPNAV N9 NAVFAC NAVSUP TFCC CNIC USA CRREL	M, F	FY14-20
2.6.5: Partner with USCG to investigate the feasibility of establishing a deep water port in the Arctic.	OPNAV N4	OPNAV N3/N5 MSC USCG	O, M, F	Q1, FY16

2.7 Platforms, Weapons, Support Equipment, and Sensors

Actions	Lead	Support	DOTMLPF	Suspense
2.7.1: Identify metrics suitable for CNO progress reports on Section 2.7 (Platforms, Weapons, Support Equipment, and Sensors) of Arctic Roadmap.	OPNAV N9	Director TFCC TFCC		Q3, FY14
2.7.2: Identify current capability of existing platforms to operate in open water (<10% sea ice) and shoulder seasons (<40% sea ice).	OPNAV N9	OPNAV N8 NAVSEA SYSCOMs	M	Q3, FY14
2.7.3: Identify future platforms and their engineering requirements that will operate in open water (<10% sea ice) and shoulder seasons (<40% sea ice) by mid 2020s. • Surface combatants • Submarines • Aviation platforms • Auxiliaries • Maritime Prepositioning Squadron Lighterage • Assault Craft Unit connectors • Coastal Riverine Craft • UUV/UAVs	OPNAV N9	OPNAV N2/N6 OPNAV N4 USFFC MSC NWDC NAVSEA SYSCOMs	M	Q3, FY14
2.7.4: Identify what platform(s) (and how many) will act as Navy's Arctic capable afloat forward staging base (AFSB) in 2020s.	OPNAV N9	OPNAV N4 OPNAV N8 CPF USFFC NAVSEA SYSCOMs	M	Q3, FY14
2.7.5: Determine if the current required operational capabilities/projected operating environment (ROC/POE) and Table of Allowance (TOA) equipage of expeditionary forces and shore based elements of other forces (e.g., shore detachments from aviation squadrons) provides the capability to support unit deployments to, and operations in, the Arctic region.	OPNAV N9	OPNAV N8 NECC SYSCOMs USFFC	M	Q3, FY14
2.7.6: Develop a plan to be prepared to execute Arctic expeditionary operations in the near term. • Based on the assessment of the existing ROC/POE and TOA of Navy units to determine which can operate in this environment already and are available on an ad hoc basis to augment units whose deficiencies place them at risk for near-term Arctic operations. • Assign one or more portions of the Navy expeditionary forces the mission of providing Combat Service Support, including camp support and the provision of expeditionary infrastructure appropriate for the Arctic environment to deploying forces.	OPNAV N9	OPNAV N8 NECC SYSCOMs USFFC	M	Q3, FY14
2.7.7: Determine a strategy for providing Naval Forces the extra TOA required for Arctic operations. Either: • Modify the TOA of eligible units to include extreme cold weather gear. • Provide a centrally managed inventory of cold weather operational support material for issue to deploying units.	OPNAV N9	OPNAV N8 NECC SYSCOMs USFFC	M	Q3, FY14

2.7.8: Evaluate requirements for sustainment of forces operating in the Arctic	OPNAV N9	OPNAV N4 OPNAV N8 CPF USFFC MSC SYSCOMs	D, O, M, T	FY14-15
2.7.9: Assess the Classified Annex to CS-21R's guidance relating to required platform, weapons, support equipment, and sensor capabilities in the Arctic, and address these requirements in Sponsor Program Proposals	OPNAV N9	OPNAV N2/N6 OPNAV N3/N5 OPNAV N4 OPNAV N8 USFFC ONR	T, M, P	FY14-20, annually
2.7.10: Evaluate requirements for expeditionary units to conduct operations in the Arctic. Environments include on ice, ashore, on permafrost, under ice diving, littoral operations and construction including underwater construction in freezing/subzero conditions. • Underwater Construction Teams • Explosive Ordnance Disposal Teams • Naval Mobile Construction Battalions • Coastal Riverine Forces • Mobile Diving and Salvage • Navy Cargo Handling Battalions	OPNAV N9	OPNAV N4 OPNAV N8 USFFC SYSCOMs	M	Q2, FY15
2.7.11: Determine weapon and sensor capabilities and requirements in an Arctic environment (surface, subsurface and aviation). • Consider ship-borne ice detecting radar requirement • Address GPS-Targeting alternatives	OPNAV N9	SYSCOMs	M	Q4, FY15

2.8 Maritime Domain Awareness

Actions	Lead	Support	DOTMLPF	Suspense
2.8.1: Identify metrics suitable for CNO progress reports on Section 2.8 (Maritime Domain Awareness) of Arctic Roadmap.	OPNAV N2/N6	Director TFCC TFCC	D	Q3, FY14
2.8.2: Ensure efforts to address JROC-validated MDA gaps account for MDA in Arctic.	OPNAV N2/N6	OPNAV N3/N5	D, O, T, M, L, P, F	Q3, FY14
2.8.3: Improve MDA through collaboration: • Influence "ad hoc" Canada/U.S. (CANUS) MDA Roundtable with USCG • Execute Information Sharing Services (developed in conjunction with the DoD Executive Agent for MDA) for use by Arctic Nations • Encourage Russia to join as a participant in the Maritime Safety & Security Information System (MSSIS) or similar system • Pursue standards-based data exchanges to share MDA data among Arctic Nations in keeping with the National MDA Architecture	OPNAV N2/N6	OPNAV N3/N5 CNE CPF USFFC ONI USCG	D, O, T, M, L, P, F	Q4, FY14 FY14-17 FY14-20 FY15-20
2.8.4: Review Classified Annex to CS-21R for guidance relating to required capabilities for MDA in the Arctic; include in Sponsor Program Proposals.	OPNAV N2/N6	OPNAV N3/N5 C6F USFFC NWDC USCG	D	FY14-15
2.8.5: Ensure data from Arctic sensors are made available to existing enterprise services/solutions.	OPNAV N2/N6	USFFC	M	FY15-18
2.8.6: Introduce common lexicon for MDA in the Arctic leveraging existing Vessel of Interest (VOI) lexicon.	OPNAV N2/N6	Director TFCC USCG	D	Q2, FY15

3.0 Build Trust and Confidence with Partners

Actions	Lead	Support	DOTMLPF	Suspense
3.1.1: Identify metrics suitable for CNO progress reports on Section 3.1 (Build Trust and Confidence with Partners) of Arctic Roadmap.	CHINFO	Director TFCC TFCC	D	Q3, FY14
3.1.2: Public Communications and Outreach. • Update Navy Arctic Public Communications Plan and review annually • Update Navy Arctic Outreach & Engagement Plan and decide on frequency of submission • Provide DOD assets with *Arctic Environmental Assessment Reports*, other TFCC products, and information and reports concerning the Arctic DOD, scientific, media, interagency, and international sources • Establish and maintain consistent outreach with, and providing information related to the Navy Arctic Roadmap • Attend relevant conferences, such as the Arctic Security Forces Roundtable (ASFR)	CHINFO	OPNAV N8 TFCC	L	Q3, FY14
• Coordinate with the Joint Staff (JSJ5) to ensure Navy representation at key Arctic meetings, conferences, etc. (e.g., Northern CHOD, ASFR)	OPNAV N3/N5			FY14-20
3.1.3: Expand cooperative partnerships with Arctic nations and Arctic states, and international, interagency and private sector stakeholders that enhance Arctic security. Focus on: • Memoranda of Agreement/Memoranda of Understanding - Pursue additional bi-lateral and multi-lateral agreements with Arctic nations to leverage capabilities and expand cooperative opportunities within the region	OPNAV N3/N5	CHINFO DUSN PPOI MSC NAVSEA NIPO NOAA NWC OJAG Code 10 ONR USCG	D, O, T, L, F	FY14-20
• Cross-Decks - Expand and formalize professional exchange programs focused on Arctic nations. (Also addressed in Operations and Training.)	Director TFCC			
• Multinational Exercise Participation – Take advantage of opportunities to participate in Arctic region exercises	USFFC			
• Facilities Access – Leverage partner nation and commercial facilities to maximum extent possible	OPNAV N4			
• Information Sharing (See 2.8.5)				
3.1.4: Confirm and codify agreements with key Arctic States.	OPNAV N3/N5	DUSN PPOI		FY14-20

4.0 Execution

Actions	Lead	Support	DOTMLPF	Suspense
4.1: Provide semi-annual reports regarding roadmap execution to CNO.	Director TFCC	TFCC	D	FY14-20
4.2: Review and revise the Navy Arctic Roadmap after promulgation of the Quadrennial Defense Review (QDR) and incorporate QDR guidance as appropriate.	Director TFCC	TFCC	D	FY14-20

Appendix 4

Glossary of Abbreviations

AFSB	Afloat Forward Staging Base
ASFR	Arcitc Security Forces Roundtable
APOD	Aerial Port of Debarkation
Arctic Council	A high-level intergovernmental forum that addresses primarily environmental protection and sustainable development issues in the Arctic region. The eight founding nations are Canada, Denmark, Finland, Iceland, Norway, Russia, Sweden and the United States.
Arctic Region	The region of the globe that consists of all U.S. and foreign territory north of the Arctic Circle and all U.S. territory north and west of the boundary formed by the Porcupine, Yukon, and Kuskokwim Rivers; all contiguous seas, including the Arctic Ocean and the Beaufort, Bering, Chukchi Seas, and the Aleutian Island chain.
ASL	Arctic Submarine Lab
ASW	Antisubmarine Warfare
C4ISR	Command, Control, Communications, Computers, Intelligence, Surveillance and Reconnaissance
C6F	Commander 6th Fleet
CANUS	Canada/United States
CBA	Capabilities Based Assessment
CHINFO	U. S. Chief of Information
CHOD	Chiefs of Defense
CIA	Central Intelligence Agency
CLCS	Commission on the Limits of the Continental Shelf
CMP	Common Maritime Picture
CNE	Commander Naval Forces Europe
CNIC	Commander Navy Installations Command
CNMOC	Commander Naval Meteorology and Oceanography Command
CNO	Chief of Naval Operations
CNR	Chief of Naval Research
COMSUBFOR	Commander, Submarine Force
CONOPS	Concept of Operations
CPF	Commander Pacific Fleet
Cross-Deck	Cross-deck (or cross-decking) is naval jargon referring to the informal, ad-hoc sharing of resources or personnel between naval vessels.
CRREL	U.S. Army Cold Regions Research and Engineering Laboratory
CS-21R	A Cooperative Strategy for 21st Century Seapower (Revised)
Destination Shipping	Intra-Arctic coastal shipping routes
DHS	Department of Homeland Security
DLA	Defense Logistics Agency
DoD	Department of Defense
DOTMLPF-P	Doctrine, Organization, Training, Materiel, Leadership and Education, Personnel and Facilities-Policy
DSCA	Defense Support of Civil Authorities
DUSN PPOI	Deputy Undersecretary of the Navy for Plans, Policy, Oversight & Integration
ECS	Extended Continental Shelf
EEZ	Exclusive Economic Zone

ESPC	Earth System Prediction Capability
EUCOM	U.S. European Command
GEF	Guidance for Employment of the Force
GPS	Global Positioning Satellite
HA/DR	Humanitarian Assistance/Disaster Response
ICEX	Ice Exercise
ILSA	International Law Students Association
IMO	International Maritime Organization
IPCC	International Panel on Climate Change
ISA	International Seabed Authority
ISR	Information, Surveillance, Reconnaissance
JROC	Joint Requirements Oversight Council
JSJ5	Joint Staff J5
LNG	Liquid Natural Gas
MDA	Maritime Domain Awareness
MEDEA	Measurements of the Earth Data for Environmental Analysis
MILSATCOM	Military Satellite Communications System
MSC	Military Sealift Command
MSSIS	Maritime Safety and Security Information System
NAVAID	Navigational Aids
Navigable Water	Defined as less than 40% ice coverage, and requiring icebreaker support
NAVSEA	Naval Sea Systems Command
NCCs	Navy Component Commands
NECC	Navy Expeditionary Combat Command
NETC	Naval Education and Training Command
NGA	National Geospatial-Intelligence Agency
NIC	National Ice Center
NIPO	Navy International Programs Office
NOAA	National Oceanic and Atmospheric Administration
NORAD	North American Aerospace Defense Command
NORTHCOM	U.S. Northern Command
NPS	Naval Post-Graduate School
NSF	National Science Foundation
NSR	Northern Sea Route
NWC	Naval War College
NWDC	Naval Warfare Development Command
NWP	Northwest Passage
OJAG	Office of the Judge Advocate General
OLA	Office of Legislative Affairs
ONI	Office of Naval Intelligence
ONR	Office of Naval Research
OPCON	Operational Control
Open Water	Defined as up to 10% of sea ice concentration with no ice of land origin (e.g., icebergs) and navigable by open oceans vessel without icebreaker escort
OPNAV	Office of the Chief of Naval Operations
OSD	Office of the Secretary of Defense
PACOM	U.S. Pacific Command
PEO C4I	Program Executive Office for Command, Control, Communications, Computers & Intelligence

POM	Program Objective Memorandum
QDR	Quadrennial Defense Review
R&D	Research and Development
S&T	Science and Technology
SAM	SCICEX Accommodation Mission
SAR	Search and Rescue
SAREX	Search and Rescue Exercise
SCICEX	Scientific Ice Exercise
Sea ice	A sheet of floating ice, chiefly on the surface of the sea, smaller than an ice field
SPAWAR	Space and Naval Warfare Systems Command
SPOD	Sea Port of Debarkation
SPP	Sponsor Program Proposal
SYSCOMs	System Commands
TFCC	Task Force Climate Change
Transit Shipping	Cross-Arctic transit routes from Europe to Asia
TRP	Transpolar Route
TYCOM	Type Commander
UAV	Unmanned Aerial Vehicle
UCP	Unified Command Plan
UNCLOS	United Nations Convention on the Law of the Sea
USAF	United States Air Force
USA	United States Army
USCG	United States Coast Guard
USFFC	Unites States Fleet Forces Command
USN	United States Navy
USNA	United States Naval Academy
UUV	Unmanned Undersea Vehicle
VOI	Vessel of Interest

[1] The Arctic nations are the standing members of the Arctic Council: Canada, Denmark (representing Greenland and the Faroe Islands), Finland, Iceland, Norway, Sweden, the Russian Federation, and the United States.

[2] The Arctic Ocean is generally taken to include Baffin Bay, Barents Sea, Beaufort Sea, Chukchi Sea, East Siberian Sea, Greenland Sea, Hudson Bay, Hudson Strait, Kara Sea, Laptev Sea, White Sea and other tributary bodies of water. It is connected to the Pacific Ocean by the Bering Strait and to the Atlantic Ocean through the Greenland Sea and Labrador Sea. <http://www.britannica.com/EBchecked/topic/33188/Arctic-Ocean> and derived from CIA World Factbook

[3] The "Arctic Region" is defined as the area that encompasses all U.S. and foreign territory north of the Arctic Circle and all U.S. territory north and west of the boundary formed by the Porcupine, Yukon, and Kuskokwim Rivers, and all contiguous seas and straits north of and adjacent to the Arctic Circle. This definition is consistent with the Arctic Research and Policy Act of 1984 (15 U.S.C. 4111) and Arctic Council usage.

[4] The Department of Defense defines the term "function" as: "The appropriate or assigned duties, responsibilities, missions, or tasks of an individual, office, or organization. As defined in the National Security Act of 1947, as amended, the term 'function' includes functions, powers, and duties (5 United States Code 171n (a))." Source: Joint Publication 1-02, *Department of Defense Dictionary of Military and Associated Terms,* as amended through 15 January 2012.

[5] The United States National Strategy for the Arctic Region, May 2013.

[6] Multi-year ice is sea ice that has survived at least one melting season (i.e., one summer). Source: Sechrist, F.S.; Fett, R.W.; Perryman, D.C., "Forecasters Handbook for the Arctic," *Naval Environmental Prediction Research Facility Technical Report* TR 89-1. 2 October 1989. Web. 17 Oct 2013. <http://www.nrlmry.navy.mil/forecaster_handbooks/Arctic/Forecasters%20Handbook%20for%20the%20Arctic.htm>

[7] Gibbs, W. "Russia and Norway Reach Accords on Barents Sea." *New York Times*. 27 April, 2010. Web. 26 Sept 2013. <http://www.nytimes.com/2010/04/28/world/europe/28norway.html?_r=0>

[8] Kraska, J. "From Pariah to Partner: Russian-American Security Cooperation in the Arctic Ocean," *ILSA Journal of International & Comparative Law* 16, no. 2 (2009), Web 3 Oct. 2013. <http://ssrn.com /abstract=1648907.>

[9] Conley, H. "Arctic Economics in the 21st Century: The Benefits and Costs of Cold." Center for Strategic and International Studies, July 2013.

[10] Budzik, P. "Arctic Oil and Natural Gas Potential." U.S. Energy Information Administration. Office of Integrated Analysis and Forecasting Oil and Gas Division. October 2009.Web. 20 Aug. 2013. <http://www.eia.gov/oiaf/analysispaper/arctic/pdf/arctic_oil.pdf>

[11] Ibid.

[12] Intelligence Community Assessment. "Military Implications of the Diminished Sea Ice in the Arctic Through 2030." ICA 2012-50. 11 July 2012.

[13] U.S. Navy. "Navy Arctic Mission Analysis." June 2011.

[14] Intergovernmental Panel on Climate Change (IPCC), *Climate Change 2007: Synthesis Report.* pg. 30 Web. 19 April, 2013. <http://www.ipcc.ch/publications_and_data/publications_ipcc_fourth_assessment_report_synthesis_report.htm>

[15] Ibid.

[16] National Snow and Ice Data Center. "Arctic Sea Ice Extent Settles at Record Seasonal Minimum." NSIDC press release. 19 Sept. 2012. Web. 20 Aug. 2013. <http://nsidc.org/arcticseaicenews/2012/09/arctic-sea-ice-extent-settles-at-record-seasonal-minimum/>

[17] Open water is defined as up to 10% of sea ice concentration with no ice of land origin (e.g. icebergs), navigable by open ocean vessels without icebreaker escort. World Meteorological Organization Pub No. 259 Sea Ice Nomenclature.

[18] "Shoulder season" is defined as less than 40 percent sea ice coverage. Task Force Climate Change (TFCC) convention.

[19] U.S. Geological Survey. "Circum-Arctic Resource Appraisal: Estimates of Undiscovered Oil and Gas North of the Arctic Circle." USGS Fact Sheet 2008 and USGS Web. 15 Aug. 2013. <http://www.usgs.gov/newsroom/article.asp?ID=1980&from=rss_home>

[20] Budzik, "Arctic Oil and Natural Gas Potential."

[21] Carmel, S. M. "The Cold Hard Realities of Arctic Shipping." *Proceedings of the Naval Institute*, Vol. 139/7/1,325. July 2013. Web. 20 Aug. 2013. <http://www.usni.org/magazines/proceedings/2013-07/cold-hard-realities-arctic-shipping>

[22] Winter, A. "U.S. Bans Commercial Fishing in Warming Arctic." *Scientific American*, 21 Aug. 2009. Web. 9 Sept 2009. <http://www.scientificamerican.com/article.cfm?id=ban-commercial-fishing-arctic-global-warming>

[23] Office of Naval Intelligence. "Geostrategic Assessments for the Arctic: Civil Maritime Activity, National Interests, and Future Trends." Briefing, July 2013.

[24] Perry, C. M. and B. Andersen. "New Strategic Dynamics in the Arctic Region." Institute for Foreign Policy Analysis. Feb. 2012. Web. 8 Oct. 2013. <http://www.ifpa.org/pdf/StrategicDynamicsArcticRegion.pdf>

[25] Budzik, "Arctic Oil and Natural Gas Potential."

[26] Office of Naval Intelligence. "Geostrategic Assessments."

[27] Institute for Foreign Policy Analysis. "New Strategic Dynamics in the Arctic Region." Feb 2012. Web. 20 Sept. 2013 <http://www.ifpa.org/pdf/StrategicDynamicsArcticRegion.pdf>

[28] "Illulissat Declaration." *Arctic Report*. Web. 18 Nov. 2013. <http://www.arctic-report.net/?post_type=products&p=859&lang=en>

[29] U.S. Department of State. Fact Sheet. "Secretary Clinton Signs the Arctic Search and Rescue Agreement with Other Arctic Nations." 12 May, 2011. Web. 9 Sept. 2013. <http://www.state.gov/r/pa/prs/ps/2011/05/163285.htm>

[30] U.S. Department of State. Fact Sheet. "Agreement on Cooperation on Marine Oil Pollution Preparedness and Response in the Arctic" 15 May, 2013. Web. 9 Sept. 2013. < http://www.state.gov/r/pa/prs/ps/2013/05/209406.htm>

[31] Office of Naval Intelligence. "Geostrategic Assessments."

[32] Exercise NORTHERN EAGLE is a biennial, combined Russian-U.S.-Norwegian naval exercise series that began in 2004. It was last held in August 2012 in the Barents Sea.

[33] Operation NANOOK is the largest Canadian Armed Forces annual exercise in Canada's North. Typically held in August, it includes multi-national participation.

[34] 10 USC § 7921.

[35] Sea Control is the employment of naval forces, supported by land and air forces as appropriate, in order to achieve military objectives in vital sea areas.

[36] Power projection is the ability of a nation to apply all or some of its elements of national power - political, economic, informational, or military – to affect outcomes.

[37] ICEX is an international exercise held every two to three years by the Navy's Arctic Submarine Lab (ASL), a Fleet Support Detachment of Commander, Submarine Forces U.S. Pacific Fleet. ASL is responsible for developing and maintaining expertise in Arctic specific skills.
Officially launched in 1994, SCICEX is a federal interagency collaboration among the operational Navy, research agencies, and the marine research community to episodically use nuclear-powered submarines for scientific studies of the Arctic Ocean.

[38] Office of Naval Intelligence. "Geostrategic Assessments."

Navy Arctic Roadmap Significant Actions

FOCUS AREA — Timeline: FY14, FY15, FY16, FY18, FY20

Strategy, Policy, Missions, & Plans
- Establish Requirements Working Group
- Advocate for Executive Agent for the Arctic
- Incorporate CS-21R guidance relating to Arctic capabilities into POM guidance
- Develop Arctic engagement plan focusing on partnerships
- Incorporate Arctic engagements in Navy Campaign Support Plan
- Develop Arctic CONOP for Naval platforms

Operations & Training
- TYCOM/s update Fleet guidance on Arctic operations
- TYCOM/s generate guidance and training requirements
- Integrate testing of sensors/systems into Arctic exercises/operations
- Increase participation/visibility in Arctic exercises

Science & Technology
- Develop personnel exchange plan with regional partners
- Incorporate Arctic related science and technology requirements in CS-21R
- Produce a holistic Arctic environmental sensing plan
- Support access to previously classified information by climate research community
- Increase ONR's Arctic Research Efforts
- Support efforts to research, develop, resource and sustain an Arctic environmental observation system in support of U.S. operations

Environmental Observation & Prediction
- Quantify and characterize uncertainty in long range climate and ice forecasting capabilities
- Develop CONOPS for Arctic environmental Observer/Forecaster support
- Sustain development of Earth System Prediction Capability Efforts (ESPC)

Safe Navigation
- Coordinate with NGA, NOAA and USCG to develop a national hydrographic plan
- Sustain Arctic Nation Navy hydrographic survey data sharing and planning effort
- Identify safe navigational corridors and NAVAID requirements

C4ISR
- Conduct analysis of existing and future high data rate communication requirements
- Establish ISR requirements for space, manned and unmanned options

Installations & Facilities
- Identify requirements to establish APODs and SPODs
- Evaluate capability of existing ports and airfields to support Navy operations

Platforms, Weapons, Support Equipment, and Sensors
- Assess current capability of existing platforms in open water/shoulder seasons
- Identify future platforms and engineering requirements that will operate in open water/shoulder seasons
- Identify platform(s) that can act as Navy's Arctic capable AFSB by mid 2020s
- Determine weapon and sensor capabilities and requirements

Maritime Domain Awareness
- Improve MDA through collaboration
- Introduce common Vessel of Interest lexicon for MDA in the Arctic

Build Trust and Confidence with Partners
- Public Communications and Outreach
- Expand cooperative partnerships with Arctic nations and Arctic states, and international, interagency and private sector stakeholders